IS Jesus
Coming Soon?

AMERICAN VISION

*"Restoring America's Biblical Foundation
from Genesis to Revelation"*

www.AmericanVision.org

American Vision, Inc.
3150-A Florence Road, Suite 2
Powder Springs, Georgia 30127-5385
1-800-628-9460
www.AmericanVision.org

DeMar, Gary.
    Is Jesus Coming Soon?
    ISBN: 0-915815-36-2

Cover art: *Hydrogen Bomb Over City* by Basil Wolverton, colorized by Monte Wolverton,
    Copyright © 1956, 1998 Worldwide Church of God. Used by permission.
Cover Design by Luis Lovelace

Is Jesus Coming Soon?

GARY DEMAR

American Vision, Inc.

P.O. Box 220 | Powder Springs, GA | 30127

CONTENTS

"The Four Horsemen of the Apocalypse." Woodcut by Albrecht Dürer (1498)

INTRODUCTION

The Olivet Discourse is found in the three synoptic Gospels: Matthew 24, Mark 13, and Luke 21. It's the largest block of prophetic material outside the Book of Revelation. Many believe Jesus is describing events in the distant future, our future. Advocates of this position are called *futurists*. Other Bible scholars, who take a more literal approach to the time texts, conclude that Jesus is addressing His contemporaries; that He is describing events that will happen to the first-century generation of Christians living in Judea. Advocates of this position are called *preterists*. Preterists believe that the fulfillment of certain prophetic texts have already occurred in events leading up to and including the destruction of Jerusalem in A.D. 70.

This first-century *preterist* coming of Christ is a coming in judgment that led to the destruction of the temple and city of Jerusalem before that first-century generation passed away (Matt. 24:34; 16:27–28). While this is neither a popular nor a well known interpretation today, the majority of conservative Bible commentators who have written on prophetic themes in the last four hundred years held this position. In fact, it can be traced back to the first, second, and third centuries.[1] Because you may not be familiar with this view, I've put this book together as an introduction. In Part One you will read a brief overview of the preterist interpretation of the Olivet Discourse. It takes you quickly through Jesus' prophecy in about ten minutes. Part Two is more detailed. Neither section, however, will answer all your questions. For a comprehensive study of the Olivet Discourse and other prophecy-related topics, see my book *Last Days Madness*.[2]

NOTES

1. Gary DeMar and Francis X. Gumerlock, *The Early Church and the End of the World* (Powder Springs, GA: American Vision, 2006).

2. Gary DeMar, *Last Days Madness: The Obsession of the Modern Church*, 4th ed. (Powder Springs, GA: American Vision, 1999).

Part One

A TEN-MINUTE GUIDE TO BIBLE PROPHECY

M Y FIRST INTRODUCTION TO Bible prophecy was through Hal Lindsey's *Late Great Planet Earth*, the publishing event of the 1970s. Lindsey presented an end-time scenario that was both fascinating and disturbing, especially to someone who knew almost nothing about the Bible. While Lindsey's prophetic novel introduced me to the Bible, I was immediately confused when I actually read God's Word and found that a number of passages he chose as the center of his system did not seem to fit the Bible's view of the end times.

If words mean anything, then Lindsey and his fellow prophecy writers are wrong. For example, how can Jack Van Impe maintain that "the rapture is near"[1] for us and ignore the plain teaching of the Bible when it emphatically states that the time for Christ's coming in judgment was "near" for the church in the first century (e.g., James 5:7–9; Rev. 1:1, 3)? How can John Van Diest, editor of *10 Reasons Why Jesus is Coming Soon*, end his introduction with this statement?: "So with the words of Jesus himself, 'Yes, I am coming *soon*' we echo with John the Apostle 'Amen. Come Lord Jesus' (Revelation 22:20)"?[2] Van Diest quotes a passage that was written nearly 2000 years ago that said that Jesus' coming was to happen "soon." Revelation says the events which are to follow "must shortly take place" (1:1), "for the time is near" (1:3; see 22:10, 12). Dave Hunt's book asks *When Will*

Jesus Come? He believes that Jesus' return will happen "soon" because in the subtitle he promises to offer *Compelling Evidence for the Soon Return of Christ*.[3] Why doesn't soon mean soon when Jesus promised to return before that first-century generation passed away nearly 2000 years ago (Matt. 24:34)? When the Bible uses words like "near," "shortly," "quickly," and "at hand," they refer to times and events that are proximate to that contemporary audience:

> The word rendered 'is at hand' . . . [in 1 Pet. 4:7] may refer either to proximity of *place or time*, and it always denotes that the *place* or the time referred to was not far off. In the former sense, as referring to nearness of place, see Matthew 21:1; Mark 11:1; Luke 7:12; 15:25; 18:35,40; 19:29,37,41; 24:46; Acts 9:3; 10:9; 21:33; in the latter sense, as referring to *time* as being near, see Matthew 3:2; Matthew 4:17; 10:7; 21:34; 26:45; Mark 1:16; Luke 21:20,28; Acts 7:17; Romans 13:12; Hebrews 10:25; 1 Peter 4:7. The idea as applied to *time*, or to *an approaching event*, is undoubtedly that it is *close by*; it is not *far off*; it will *soon occur*.[4]

A Prophetic Pilgrimage

At first reading, the New Testament seems to teach that the temple would be destroyed (Matt. 23:38; 24:2), Jerusalem would come under siege (Matt. 22:7), and the Old Covenant order would come to an end before the last disciple died (Matt. 10:23; 16:27–28; cf. John 21:18–23). Jesus prophesied that a series of devastating events would take place before that first-century generation passed away (Matt. 24:34). But how could this be? Lindsey and other prophecy writers presented what seemed to be compelling evidence that "famines, pestilences, and earthquakes" (24:7), the rise of "false prophets" (24:11), and the gospel being preached "to all the nations" (24:14) were end-time events that were taking place in *our* day. I was confused.

I looked for an answer in the Bible. Steadily, I began to see that the Bible really is its own best interpreter. Jesus said there would be famines before the generation to whom He was speaking would pass away. A famine hit the Roman Empire "in the days of Claudius Caesar" (Acts 11:28), who ruled from A.D. 41 to 54. Luke describes the famine as being "throughout all the world," that is, encompassing the borders of the Roman Empire since the Greek word *oikoumene* ("inhabited earth" or "known world") and not *kosmos* ("world") is used.

Map of the Roman Empire

Was the "gospel of the kingdom preached in all the *world* for a witness to all the nations" prior to the destruction of the temple in A.D. 70? I learned that the Greek word translated "world" in Matthew 24:14 is the same Greek word used in Luke 2:1 to describe a "world-wide" census that took place during the time of Jesus' birth and is best translated "inhabited earth" or "known world" (cf. Acts 11:28). Paul states unequivocally that the gospel *"was preached to every creature under heaven"* (Col. 1:23) in *his* day. The gospel had "been made known to all nations" in *his* day (Rom. 16:26). Those who are mesmerized by end-time speculation will insist that this did not happen. Their argument is with the Bible, not me. Paul's language is clear.

Of course, those who claim that Jesus did not teach His soon coming in judgment upon Jerusalem follow in the steps of liberals who have claimed that Jesus and the writers of the New Testament were mistaken about the timing of prophetic events. Here's one example:

> The content of this revelation, given by God to Jesus Christ, had to do with "what must soon take place." If we take this to mean that persecution will increase and Christians need to be prepared for it, then he was certainly proven right by later events. On the other hand, John apparently expected the total fulfillment of God's plan to take place in the near future, and in that case he was mistaken.[5]

Jesus and the New Testament writers were not mistaken. After a prolonged and careful study, I found that each and every prophetic event outlined by Jesus in the Olivet Discourse took place prior to the destruction of Jerusalem in A.D. 70.

I soon became aware of first-century secular sources that supported the Bible's prophetic record without ever referencing the Bible. Keep in mind that all the New Testament books were written prior to A.D. 70, therefore, we do not have an *inspired* historical narrative of the siege of Jerusalem and the destruction of the temple. Even so, these eye-witness accounts are helpful and lend support to the biblical record.

One of the most difficult passages to reconcile with an A.D. 70 fulfillment is Jesus' statement that before that first-century generation passed away the tribes of Israel "will see the Son of Man coming on the clouds of heaven with power and great glory" (24:30). Jesus offers the same prophecy to those who witnessed His trial before Caiaphas the high priest: "*You* will see the Son of Man sitting at the right hand of the Power, and coming on the clouds of heaven" (Matt. 26:64). The language seems to suggest that those alive and well in the first century would see this event.

A BROTHER'S CONFIRMATION

Is there any evidence that those who walked with Jesus applied the fulfillment of these passages to their generation? James, the brother of Jesus, identifies the coming of Jesus "on the clouds of heaven" with events that were to take place soon, possibly within his lifetime. The fourth-century church historian Eusebius writes in his *Ecclesiastical History* that when asked about the coming of

Church historian Eusebius of Caesarea (c. 263–339)

the Son of Man, James responded, quoting the words of Jesus recorded for us in Matthew 24:30 and 26:64, that "He is now sitting in the heavens, on the right hand of great Power, and *is about to*

The martyrdom of James, the brother of Jesus

come on the clouds of heaven." After hearing this, the officials of the temple cast him down from the "wing of the temple" and beat out his brains with a club.[6] The martyrdom of James occurred around A.D. 62. Soon after the death of James, Vespasian invaded and took Judea. Seven years later the temple was destroyed in the way Jesus said it would be (Matt. 24:2). James' use of this "end-time" passage supports the New Testament's claim and the early church's belief that Jesus' "coming on the clouds of heaven" was near *for them*. "Coming on the clouds" is a descriptive metaphor that refers to exaltation and kingly ascension which applies to Jesus (Dan. 7:13–14).

THE HISTORICAL RECORD

The majority of today's prophecy writers see today's "wars and rumors of wars" as clear evidence that we are living in the last days. A study of the period before Jerusalem's destruction in A.D. 70 tells a different story. The Roman historian Tacitus (A.D. 56–117) writes in his history of the period that there were "disturbances in Germany," "commotions in Africa," "commotions in Thrace," "insurrections in Gaul," "intrigues among the Parthians," a "war in Britain," and a "war in Armenia." Wars were fought from one end of the empire to the other in a time of supposed peace.

The Jewish historian Josephus (*c.* A.D. 30–100), an eyewitness to the Roman destruction of Jerusalem, writes that Roman civil wars were so common in the empire that there was no need to write about them in any great detail: "I have omitted to give an exact account of them, because they are well known by all, and they are described by a great number of Greek and Roman authors."

Flavius Josephus (c. A.D. 30–100)

In Luke 21:11 we are told that "there will be fearful sights and great signs from heaven." The historical record shows that a comet appeared around A.D. 60. Comets were thought to be omens of

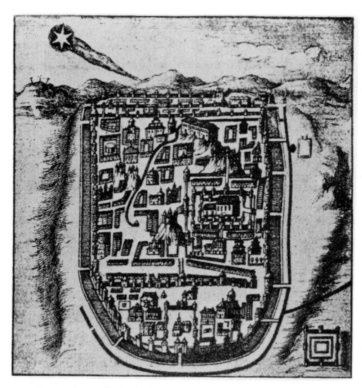

Depiction of Halley's Comet over Jerusalem (A.D. 66)

doom. Nero took the comet's threat seriously and had members of his own family killed in case they saw the stellar phenomenon as a heavenly sign from the gods to dethrone him. Halley's Comet appeared in A.D. 66 and was "later said to be a warning of the fall of Jerusalem to the Romans in A.D. 70."[7] In addition to Halley's Comet, Josephus recounts that "there was a star resembling a sword, which stood over the city, and a comet, that continued a whole year."

Is there any historical evidence that "power, signs, and lying wonders" (2 Thess. 2:9) took place just prior to Jerusalem's destruction?

And what about the appearance of "false christs and false prophets" (Matt. 24:24)? Josephus supports the biblical prophetic record when he reports:

> And now these impostors and deceivers persuaded the multitude to follow them into the wilderness, and pretended that they would *exhibit manifest wonders and signs*, that should be performed by the providence of God. . . . Moreover, there came out of Egypt about this time to Jerusalem, one that said he was a prophet, and advised the multitude of the common people to go along with him to the Mount of Olives. . . . He said that he would show them from hence, how, at his command, the walls of Jerusalem would fall down; and he promised that he would procure them an entrance into the city through those walls, when they were fallen down.

In another place Josephus tells of a false prophet "who had made a public proclamation in the city . . . that God commanded them to get up upon the temple, and that there they should receive miracu-

First-century Jerusalem

9

lous signs of their deliverance." Eschatological expectation intensified as Jerusalem's war with Rome came to a head. Many believed that the Messiah would return to deliver them. False prophets took advantage of this spurious expectation and deceived many. To these unbelievers, the expected deliverer had not come, so they looked for any hint of hope in a political deliverer.

The temple, with its animal sacrifices, officiated over by sinful priests, was gone. The Messiah had come in the Person of Jesus Christ seventy years before. He is "the temple" (John 2:21); "the lamb of God who takes away the sin of the world" (1:29); a "High Priest forever according to the order of Melchizedek" (Heb. 6:20). Jerusalem, the city of Old Covenant redemption, was replaced by the "heavenly Jerusalem," the "city of the living God" (12:22). What does this mean for us? "But now He has obtained a more excellent ministry, inasmuch as He is also the Mediator of a better covenant, which was established on better promises" (8:6).

NOTES

1.   Jack Van Impe, *The Great Escape: Preparing for the Rapture, the Next Event on God's Prophetic Clock* (Nashville, TN: Word, 1998), 146.

2.   John Van Diest, ed., *10 Reasons Why Jesus Is Coming Soon: Ten Christian Leaders Share Their Insight* (Sisters, OR: Multnomah, 1998), 8.

3.   Dave Hunt, *When Will Jesus Come?: Compelling Evidence for the Soon Return of Christ* (Eugene, OR: Harvest House, [1993], 2003).

4.   Albert Barnes, *Notes on the New Testament: 1 Peter* (Grand Rapids, MI: Baker Book House, [1884–1885]), 193.

5.   Catherine Gunsalus Gonzalez and Justo L. Gonzalez, *Revelation* (Louisville, Kentucky: Westminster John Knox Press, 1997), 12.

6.   William Cave, *Antiquitates Apostolicae or, the History of the Lives, Acts and Martyrdoms of the Holy Apostles of Our Saviour* (London: R. Norton, 1672), 193.

7.   Isaac Asimov, *Asimov's Guide to Halley's Comet: The Awesome Story of Comets* (New York: Walker and Company, 1985), 6.

Part Two

TIMING THE GREAT TRIBULATION

A PRETERIST PERSPECTIVE OF MATTHEW 24:1–34

MATTHEW 24:1–34 IS A key prophetic passage, and its interpretation is one of the most hotly debated subjects in "end times" discussions. The purpose of this book is to encourage Christians to look at the plain teaching of the Bible regarding this and other prophetic texts. We must put aside our preconceived interpretations and let the Bible interpret the Bible. After all, this is the only acceptable approach to take when trying to understand any part of God's Word.

When we study Matthew 24 in its biblical context and allow other passages to shape our understanding, we will have no other choice than to embrace a *preterist* interpretation. *Preterism* teaches that most prophetic passages in the New Testament—including Matthew 24:1–34—were fulfilled in the destruction of Jerusalem in A.D. 70. Preterism simply means "events that took place in the *past*." While the events described by Jesus on the Mount of Olives were future to those who first heard His words, they are fulfilled prophecy for us. There can be no doubt that the fall of Jerusalem was a key eschatological event in biblical history. It marked the end of the old covenant order—the end of the temple, temple sacrifices, and the old-covenant priesthood—and the beginning of the new covenant order in Jesus.

It is important to consider all prophecy, including Matthew 24, in light of the larger covenantal picture. Throughout the Old Testament, God made covenants with His people: if they were faithful He would be a God to them and their children. God would protect and provide for them, and they were required to obey Him and trust in His promises—chief of which was His promise of a coming Redeemer. Jesus came to earth as the fulfillment of all the messianic prophecies (Luke 24:27, 44–49). He was the Savior whom faithful Israelites believed in and anticipated for centuries (2:25–38). Yet,

"Give us Barabbas" (Luke 23:18)

at the time of Jesus' earthly ministry, many of the Jewish leadership had become apostate. Throughout the gospels, most of Jesus' anger is directed at those who had rejected Him and His commandments by establishing a set of laws designed by man that had the effect of setting aside "the commandments of God" (Mark 7:1–13). The ultimate rejection came, of course, when "the chief priests and the elders persuaded the multitudes to ask for Barabbas, and to put

"Behold the man," says Pilate (John 19:5)

Jesus to death" (Matt. 27:20). To add insult to injury, when given the opportunity to embrace Jesus as their king, the chief priests cried out to Pontius Pilate, "We have no king but Caesar" (John 19:15).

Those who had broken God's covenant and had become spiritually bankrupt would be judged if they did not embrace Jesus as the promised Messiah. God would cut off apostate Judaism and give

His kingdom to "a nation producing the fruit of it" (Matt. 21:43). John the Baptist led the way with his indictment of the self-righteous religious leaders of his day:

> But when he saw many of the Pharisees and Sadducees coming for baptism, he said to them, "You brood of vipers, who warned you to flee from the wrath to come? Therefore bring forth fruit in keeping with your repentance; and do not suppose that you can say to yourselves, 'We have Abraham for our father'; for I say to you, that God is able from these stones to raise up children to Abraham. And the axe is already laid at the root of the trees. . . . And His winnowing fork is in His hand, and He will thoroughly clean His threshing floor; and He will gather His wheat into the barn, but He will burn up the chaff with unquenchable fire (Matt. 3:7–12).

There are numerous other prophetic statements in the gospels regarding Jerusalem's soon demise (see Matt. 21:33–46; 22:1–14; and 23:31–38). Jesus Himself prophesied that He would return in judgment before that first-century generation passed away to bring judgment on the nation that had rejected Him. Later, after Jesus' death and resurrection, the church was continually warned to be ready for the wrath to come, but many Jewish leaders continued to reject Jesus and persecute His church. Paul spoke of these Jews as those who "always fill up the measure of their sins" and upon whom "the wrath has come . . . to the utmost" (1 Thess. 2:16). Many verses in the New Testament point to a dramatic and earth-shaking series of events that the first-century world would soon experience (Rom. 12:11–12; 1 Cor. 7:26, 29–31; Col. 3:6; Heb. 10:25, 37; James 5:8–9; 1 Peter 4:5, 7; 1 John 2:17–18). The judgment against apostate Judaism culminated in the fall of Jerusalem in A.D. 70.

The view of prophecy that is most popular today is dispensational premillennialism, the belief that the Bible is split up into a variety of "dispensations" and that most prophetic passages in the Bible refer to a time still in our future. Modern dispensational scholars like to argue that their prophetic teachings are as old as the

Cyrus Ingerson Scofield (1843–1912)

hills, and that preterism is the wild, new kid on the prophetic block. But a survey of Bible commentators will prove that the reverse is true. Dispensationalism is relatively new and has become popular only within the last one hundred years with the publication of the *Scofield Reference Bible* which first appeared in 1909 and was revised in 1917.[1]

On the other hand, preterism—the belief that key New Testament prophecies were fulfilled in the first century—is by far the dominant eschatological perspective within the whole history of the church. A simple examination of the way Bible commentators have interpreted Matthew 24 throughout church history will show that for centuries the phrase "this generation" in Matthew

23:36 and 24:34 was interpreted as the generation of Jesus' day, not a distant generation. In addition, these commentators understood that all the events prior to Matthew 24:34 referred to events leading up to and including the destruction of Jerusalem in A.D. 70:

- Henry Hammond (1653): "I now assure you, that in the age of some that are now alive, shall all that has been said in this chapter be certainly fulfilled."[2]

John Lightfoot (1602–1675)

- John Lightfoot (1658): "Hence it appears plain enough, that the foregoing verses [Matt. 24:1–34] are not to be understood of the last judgment, but, as we said, of the destruction of Jerusalem. There were some among the disciples (particularly John), who lived to see these things come to pass. With Matt. xvi. 28, compare John xxi. 22. And there were some Rabbins [*sic*] alive at the time when Christ spoke these things, that lived until the city was destroyed."[3]

- Philip Doddridge (1750): "And *verily I say unto you*; and urge you to observe it, as absolutely necessary in order to understand what I have been saying, *That this generation* of men now living *shall not pass away until all these things be fulfilled*, for what I have foretold concerning the destruction of the Jewish state is so near at hand, that some of you shall live to see it all accomplished with a dreadful exactness."[4]

Thomas Newton
(1704–1782)

- Thomas Newton (1755): "It is to me a wonder how any man can refer part of the foregoing discourse to the destruction of Jerusalem, and part to the end of the world, or any other distant event, when it is said so positively here in the conclusion, *All these things shall be fulfilled in this generation*."[5]

- John Gill (1766): "This is a full and clear proof, that not any thing that is said before [v. 34], relates to the second coming of Christ, the day of judgment, and the end of the world; but that all belongs to the coming of the son of man in the destruction of Jerusalem, and to the end of the Jewish state."[6]

- Thomas Scott (1817): "This absolutely restricts our primary interpretation of the prophecy to the destruction of Jerusalem, which took place within forty years."[7]

Identifying the Time: "*This* Generation"

Many dispensationalists assume that Matthew 24:1–34 describes a distant future tribulation, rapture, and physical return of Christ. This is a convenient interpretation for those who hold to a future orientation for all prophetic passages in Scripture. Upon close examination, it does not hold true to the plain meaning of the passage. It is critical that we allow the time texts of Matthew 23:26 and 24:34 to be our interpretive guide. We must let the Bible define terms and phrases, and, in so doing, we will see that this entire section fits clearly within an A.D. 70 fulfillment time frame.

Like all of Scripture, Matthew 24 cannot be understood fully without surveying its context which flows from chapter 23. Keep in mind that in the original manuscripts of the Bible, there are no chapter and verse divisions. In the Greek text, chapter 24 follows immediately after chapter 23. Furthermore, the prophetic words Jesus spoke in chapter 24 are directly related to the events described in chapter 23. The disciples had just heard Jesus pronounce "woes" on the scribes and Pharisees who "have seated themselves in the chair of Moses" (23:13, 14, 15, 16, 23, 25, 27, 29). Jesus ended with this bombshell: "Behold, *your house* is being left to you desolate!" (Matt. 23:38). Chapter 24 begins with, "Jesus came out from the temple and was going away when His disciples came up to point out the temple building to Him" (24:1). So then, the "house" that would be left "desolate" was the first-century temple that had been rebuilt under the direction of Herod the Great. The disciples were obviously shocked. That's why they asked Jesus, "When will these things happen, and what will be the sign of Your coming, and of the end of the age?" (24:3). The disciples equated the destruction of the temple with the coming of Jesus and the end of the age.

Jesus' answer to this question must be understood in light of what He had said in the previous chapter. The subject and audience have not changed. Jesus had just told the scribes and Pharisees, "Truly I say to *you*, all these things will come upon *this generation*" (23:36). Jesus and His disciples were discussing questions related to the time and signs of Jerusalem's destruction since that was the

"The Two Covenants" (Gal. 4:21–31)

topic of discussion. Many of the influential religious leaders would reject Jesus as the Christ, and so they would be judged, and the Old Covenant order would end with the destruction of Jerusalem. This would be the "sign" of the "end of the age [*aion*]" of the Old Covenant and the consummation of the New Covenant.

The time text of "this generation" found in Matthew 23:36 and 24:34 is critical to the proper understanding of this prophecy. These two texts form eschatological bookends for this study.

- "Truly I say to you, all these things will come upon this generation" (23:36).

- "Truly I say to you, this generation will not pass away until all these things take place" (24:34).

Jesus preaching

Sandwiched between these two time texts are the "sign" texts, the verses that describe the signs leading up to the temple's destruction, the end of the age, and Jesus' judgment-coming on Jerusalem that would take place before that first-century generation passed away. Dispensationalists do not believe that the phrase "this generation" refers to the generation to whom Jesus was speaking but rather to some future generation. There are a number of problems with this position.

First, projecting this passage into a future fulfillment ignores its clear, literal interpretation. Jesus said, "*this* generation will not pass away until *all these things* take place." Some try to get around the clear meaning of the phrase by claiming that there was a partial fulfillment in A.D. 70 but there will be a greater or secondary fulfillment sometime in our future. This is not the plain and literal reading of the text. "All these things" were clearly to take place within the "this generation" time frame. The text does not support the interpretation that there is a gap between the A.D. 70 events and some future events two thousand years from the time when Jesus first made the prophecy. "This generation" and "all these things" are tied together. There is nothing in the Olivet Discourse to lead us to believe in some type of "double fulfillment" where these events repeat themselves in a future tribulational period with a rebuilt temple.

Second, whenever Jesus uses the phrase "this generation," it always means the generation to whom Jesus is speaking. Those who deny this must maintain that in this one instance the phrase means something different from the way it is used in every other place in Matthew and in the other Gospels. The "this generation" of Matthew 23:36 clearly has reference to the Pharisees and their contemporary generation. Why should we interpret "this generation" in Matthew 24:34 any differently, especially since Jesus was answering His disciples' question regarding their generation and the scribes and Pharisees Jesus had just condemned?

Whenever the phrase "this generation" is used in the Gospels, it means that contemporary generation. It never means "race" (*genos*), as some dispensationalists claim, since the Greek word *genea* is used and is translated elsewhere as "generation." Here is a list of every occurrence of "generation" and **"this generation"** in the Gospels: Matthew 1:16; **11:16**; 12:39; **41, 42,** 45; 16:4; 17:17; **23:36**; **24:34**; Mark **8:12**, 38; 9:19; **13:30**; Luke 1:48, 50; **7:31**; 9:41; **11:29, 30, 31, 32, 50, 51**; 16:8; **17:25**; **21:32**. In each case, these verses describe events that apply to that first-century generation.

Third, notice how many times Jesus uses the word "you" in the parallel passage in Luke 21:12: "They will lay their hands on *you* and persecute *you*, delivering *you* to the synagogues and prisons, bringing *you* before kings and governors for My name's sake" (see verses 13–20, 28, and 30). Luke 21, Matthew 24, and Mark 13 are all parallel passages in that they describe the same set of events in the same period of time, and they all use language that indicates fulfillment within the first century A.D.

Thomas Ice and Tim LaHaye claim that Matthew 24:34 should be read this way: "**The** generation **that 'sees' these things** will not pass till all is fulfilled."[8] Notice that they substitute "the" for the near demonstrative "this" which changes the focus of the passage from a specific generation—*"this* generation"— to any generation *but* the generation to whom Jesus was speaking. "This" always refers to something that is near, either in time or distance. To complicate things further, Tim LaHaye's *Prophecy Study Bible* includes this comment on Matthew 24:34: **"This generation will not pass."** This is a reference to the future generation that will live to see all the signs listed in the previous verses fulfilled in their lifetime."[9] As we've seen, "this generation" is never used to describe a future generation. Jesus tells His first-century, then-present audience which generation will "see all the signs listed in the previous verses": "even so *you* too, when *you see* all *these things*, recognize that He is near, right at the door" (Matt. 24:33). The use of "you" throughout chapter 24 refers to the audience to whom Jesus was speaking not some non-specific future audience. If Jesus wanted to designate a future audience, Matthew 24:34 would read as follows: "*That* generation will not pass away until all *those* things take place." Furthermore, Jesus would have used "they" instead of "you" (24:2, 4, 5, 6, 9, 15, 20, 23, 26, 33).

Fourth, notice that Jesus warned His followers to flee *Judea* when they saw the fulfillment of the events He described. This warning clearly applies to the destruction of Jerusalem in A.D. 70. Jesus warned His people that when they would see the increase of persecution by the Romans, and when they would see the Roman armies descend upon Jerusalem, they should flee the imminent "great tribulation" (Luke 21:20).

AN EXPOSITION OF MATTHEW 24:1–34

As we go through this passage, consider these verses from the perspective of Jesus' disciples, the original audience. What would they have thought Jesus was talking about? What conclusion would they have drawn other than a realization that judgment was going to come upon their generation? Would they have jumped to the conclusion that Jesus was talking about some generation in the distant future? It is far more likely that they would have been impressed by the impending nature of the coming tribulation. The study that follows is a verse by verse analysis of this important chapter.

> **Jesus came out from the temple and was going away when His disciples came up to point out the temple buildings to Him. And He said to them, "Do you not see all these things? Truly I say to you, not one stone here will be left upon another, which will not be torn down." Matthew 24:1–2**

When Jesus' disciples heard His prediction about the "desolation" of the temple and city in Matthew 23, they "came up to point out the temple buildings to Him," as if to say, "Lord, you can't mean *this* temple!" But Jesus confirmed His earlier announcement of impending judgment by declaring that "not one stone *here* shall be left upon another, which will not be torn down." Jesus was not describing what would happen to some future rebuilt temple. He was speaking about the destruction of the very temple that stood before them *at that time*. Probably stunned at this point, the disciples asked Jesus a multi-faceted question:

> **As He was sitting on the Mount of Olives, the disciples came to Him privately, saying, "Tell us, when will these things happen, and what will be the sign of Your coming, and of the end of the age?" Matthew 24:3**

Jesus and His disciples on the Mount of Olives

The disciples' question involves a number of interrelated events: the time of the temple's destruction and the signs that would signal Jesus' coming in judgment that would bring an end to their age (cf. 1 Cor. 10:11; Heb. 1:1–2). The disciples linked the "end of the age" with Jesus' coming: "This last phrase is governed by a single definite article in Greek, which indicates that the 'coming' (*parousia*) and the 'close of the age' are descriptions of the same event."[10]

The disciples were amazed by this prophecy that the temple and everything the temple embodied—the priesthood, the sacrifices, and the whole Jewish economy—would soon come to an end. Their questions could not have referred to Jesus' Second Coming, as some claim. Why would they be asking about a distant physical coming of Jesus on clouds to the earth when they still did not grasp the significance of His first coming that included His death, resurrection, and ascension?

The disciples clearly equated the destruction of the temple with Jesus' "coming" in judgment and with "the end of the age." The destruction of the temple would dramatically mark the end of the Old Covenant redemptive system with its sacrifices and rituals. From the very beginning, these rituals were only symbols of the coming atoning work of Christ, and the Perfect Lamb of God would render temple sacrifices totally unnecessary. "End of the age" is a covenantal phrase. It refers to the termination of the exclusive Jewish entitlement to covenant promises and the inclusion of Gentiles into the blessings of the covenant (see also Matt. 21:41, 43; 22:10). Under the New Covenant, the temple was replaced by the body of Jesus Christ (John 2:19–22) and by the church (2 Cor. 6:16).

How is it possible that Jesus "came" in A.D. 70? We must allow Scripture to interpret Scripture and evaluate what "coming" means in parallel passages. Throughout the Old Testament, God "came" in judgment (Gen. 11:5; Ex. 3:8; 19:9; 34:5; Psalm 18:6–17; 72:6; 104:3; Isa. 19:1–4; 31:4; Micah 1:3–5; Mal. 3:5). In addition, the New

Testament speaks of Jesus' coming in judgment (Matt. 10:23; 16:27–28; 26:27–28; 26:64; Mark 14:61–62). Notice how many times Jesus threatens to judge the churches of Asia Minor by His coming (Rev. 2:5, 16; 3:3). It makes no sense if the coming referred to in these

The death of the Apostle Peter (John 21:18–19)

verses is a future *distant* coming. The threatened comings are local and particular to a certain period of time and place.

Furthermore, Jesus constantly states that His coming in judgment was "near." In fact, Matthew 16:27–28 tells us that His judgment would come before the last apostle died: "For the Son of Man is going to come in the glory of His Father with His angels, and will then repay every man according to his deeds. Truly I say to you, *there are some of those who are standing here who will not taste death until they see the Son of Man coming in His kingdom.*" Peter certainly understood that Jesus' coming was near. He specifically asked whether

John would be alive when Jesus came (John 21:21–22). It was Peter who wrote in his first epistle that he was writing in the "last times" (1 Peter 1:20) and that the "end of all things was at hand" (4:7).

After the disciples asked Jesus these questions about when He would come in judgment, He answered with specific instructions:

And Jesus answered and said to them, "See to it that no one misleads you. For many will come in My name, saying, 'I am the Christ,' and will mislead many. You will be hearing of wars and rumors of wars. See that you are not frightened, for those things must take place, but that is not yet the end. For nation will rise against nation, and kingdom against kingdom, and in various places there will be famines and earthquakes. But all these things are merely the beginning of birth pangs." Matthew 24:4–8

The first item to notice in Jesus' words is that He was clearly addressing His present listeners and warning them about the events surrounding the destruction of the temple that was standing before them. "See that no one misleads *you*." *They* would be hearing of "wars and rumors of wars. . . . See that *you* are not frightened." The *disciples* would be delivered up to tribulation: "They will kill *you*," and "*you* will be hated." The logic is obvious: Jesus' warning was to the generation of disciples who asked the question about the coming judgment.

Second, Jesus warned His followers to be on the lookout for signs that were a prelude to His coming in judgment. The signs were common. He warned them that they would see false messiahs, wars and rumors of wars, famines, and earthquakes. As we briefly look at each one of these specific signs, we will see how clearly all these prophecies were fulfilled in the generation after Jesus first spoke these words on Mount Olivet.

Jesus warned His disciples to beware of false messiahs. We know from later Bible texts, as well as from secular histories of that time, that false messiahs did indeed come on the scene early in the church's history. The book of Acts gives us several examples. One such false messiah, Judas of Galilee, "rose up in the days of the census and drew away some people after him" (Acts 5:37). Another false christ described in Acts is Simon who claimed to be called "the Great Power of God" (Acts 8:9–11; see 5:36 and 13:6). Historians such as Eusebius and Josephus also record the emergence of false messiahs during the first-century A.D. Eusebius speaks of "certain men were suborned by demons as their agents, who said they were gods. . . . Simon, a certain Samaritan of the village called Githon, was one of the number, who, in the reign of Claudius Caesar, performed many magic rites by the operation of demons, was considered a god." Josephus refers to "a certain imposter named Theudas [who] persuaded a great number to follow him to the river Jordan which he claimed would divide for their passage."[11] There were so many of these imposters preying on the gullibility of the people that under the procuratorship of Felix, "many of them were apprehended and killed every day. They seduced great numbers of the people still expecting the Messiah."[12] Even dispensationalist author Larry Spargimino admits "there were other periods of woe for the city of Jerusalem that brought untold misery to the people. And false messiahs were not limited to the first century."[13]

Jesus next warned of "wars and rumors of wars" and the rising of "kingdom against kingdom." Just as He predicted, turmoil was widespread throughout that generation. The *Annals of Tacitus*, covering the period from A.D. 14 to the death of Nero in A.D. 68, describes the tumult of the period with phrases such as "disturbances in Germany," "commotions in Africa," "commotions in Thrace," "insurrections in Gaul," "intrigues among the Parthians," "the war in Britain," and "the war in Armenia." Wars were fought from one end of the empire to the other. All this took place during the *Pax Romana*, the Roman Peace. Wars are not signs except during a time of declared peace.

Christ also told His disciples that famines in the land would signify the drawing near to judgment. Were there famines during this forty year period? Indeed there were. Beginning with the Book of Acts, we see that famines were prevalent in the period prior to Jerusalem's destruction in A.D. 70. "Now at this time some prophets

A woman resorts to eating her own child because of the great famine

came down from Jerusalem to Antioch. And one of them named Agabus stood up and began to indicate by the Spirit that there would certainly be a great famine all over the world [Greek: *oikoumene*]. And this took place in the reign of Claudius. And in the proportion that any of the disciples had means, each of them determined to send a contribution for the relief of the brethren living in Judea" (Acts 11:27–29). The famine was so great that the church as far away as Corinth participated in relief efforts (1 Cor. 16:1–5; Rom. 15:25–28). The entire Roman Empire was affected.

In addition, secular historians attest to the fact that there were famines during that period. Tacitus writes about the year A.D. 51: "This year witnessed many . . . repeated earthquakes . . . a shortage of corn, resulting in famine. . . . It was established that there was no more than fifteen days' supply of food in the city [of Rome]."[14] Josephus also reports on the miserable famine conditions brought

Tacitus (A.D. 55–118)

on by the siege of Jerusalem by Titus: "Then did the famine widen its progress, and devoured the people by whole houses and families; the upper rooms were full of women and children that were dying by famine; and the lanes of the city were full of the dead bodies of the aged; the children also and the young men wandered about the marketplaces like shadows, all swelled with the famine, and fell down dead wheresoever their misery seized them."[15] All these reports were dramatic evidence to the disciples that Jesus' prophecy was coming to pass in their generation, just like He said it would.

In Matthew 24:7 Jesus also spoke of earthquakes that would proceed the fall of Jerusalem. Acts records that there was "a great earthquake" that shook "the foundations of the prison house" (Acts 16:26). According to historical accounts, this was not a rare occurrence for that time. Rather, a staggering number of earthquakes took place throughout the Roman Empire in the period before A.D. 70. Josephus writes that earthquakes were common calamities, and he describes one earthquake in Judea of such magnitude "that the constitution of the universe was confounded for the destruction of men."[16]

A great deal of attention has been focused on the number of hurricanes that struck the United States in 2005 and the tsunami that hit Asia in 2004. Many believe that these are signs of the end based on Luke's account of the Olivet Discourse where he writes about the "perplexity at the roaring of the sea and the waves" (Luke 21:25). The Mediterranean Sea floor is littered with ships that broke apart and sank because of storms. We read of one such incident in Acts 27.

The shipwreck experience of the Apostle Paul (Acts 27:14–44)

The storm is described as a "Euraquilo," that is, "a northeaster" (27:14). Luke writes that they did not see the sun or stars "for many days" (27:20). The ship finally ran aground where it was "broken up by the force of the waves" (27:41). The Roman historian Tacitus describes a series of similar events in A.D. 65:

> The Gods also marked by storms and diseases a year made shameful by so many crimes. Campania was devastated by a hurricane. . . the fury of which extended to the vicinity of the City, in which a violent pestilence was carrying away every class of human beings . . . houses were filled with dead bodies, the streets with funerals.[17]

The natural disasters described by Matthew, Mark, and Luke, common to every age, pointed specifically to the coming of Jesus in judgment upon Jerusalem before that first-century generation passed away.

"Then they will deliver you to tribulation, and will kill you, and you will be hated by all nations because of My name. At that time many will fall away and will betray one another and hate one another. Many false prophets will arise and will mislead many. Because lawlessness is increased, most people's love will grow cold." Matthew 24:9–12

Jesus continued His warnings to His disciples by telling them that during the time span of "this generation" they would see escalating crises: tribulation, falling away and betrayal, false prophets, and increased lawlessness.

No one can doubt that persecution followed believers in Jesus soon after Pentecost. Jesus warned His disciples that those who hated Him would hate them as well (John 15:18; Matt. 23:34). From its inception the church underwent relentless tribulation. Peter and John were arrested and put in jail (Acts 4:3). They were warned not to speak to any man in the name of Jesus (4:17). They were arrested again and, when released, were "flogged" (5:40).

The tribulation worsened with the death of Stephen (7:54–60). At that time, "a great persecution began against the church in Jerusalem, and they were all scattered throughout the regions

The stoning of Stephen
(Acts 7:54–60)

of Judea and Samaria, except the apostles" (8:1). Before too long, crowds turned against the disciples in frenzied persecution: "Jews came from Antioch and Iconium, and having won over the crowds, they stoned Paul and dragged him out of the city, supposing him to be dead" (14:19). Paul himself wrote, "Five times I received from the Jews thirty-nine lashes. Three times I was beaten with rods, once I was stoned. . . . I have been on frequent journeys, in dangers from rivers, dangers from robbers, dangers from my countrymen, dangers from the Gentiles . . . dangers from false brethren" (2 Cor. 11:24–26). Throughout the New Testament, we see that Jesus' disciples were delivered up to tribulation, and some were killed (Matt. 24:9). The apostle John wrote that he was a "fellow partaker *in the tribulation*" (Rev. 1:9).

There is no doubt that the first-century church had to contend with betrayal and apostasy from within, as Jesus had said: "many will fall away and will betray one another" (Matt. 24:10). Some who once proclaimed the name of Christ went on to do harm to the church they formerly claimed as their own. Paul stated, "All who are in Asia turned away from me, among whom are Phygelus and Hermogenes" (2 Tim. 1:15). Demas, who was said to have "loved this present world," deserted Paul (4:10). This apostasy does not seem to have been an isolated event: "At my first defense no one supported me, but all deserted me; may it not be counted against them" (4:16). There were also Judaizers who were constantly

The Apostle Peter

distorting the gospel and preaching doctrine that opposed "the gospel of Christ" (Gal. 1:6–10).

The Apostle Peter wrote that "false prophets also arose among the people, *just as there will also be false teachers among you, who will secretly introduce destructive heresies, even denying the Master who bought them, bringing swift destruction upon themselves*" (2 Peter 2:1). Paul also described the Judaizing teachers as "false apostles, deceitful workers, disguising themselves as apostles of Christ" (2 Cor. 11:13). The first-century church was warned that "savage wolves will come in among *you*, not sparing the flock; and from among your own selves men will arise, speaking perverse things, to draw away the disciples after them" (Acts 20:29–30).

Some false prophets were singled out for condemnation, such as Hymenaeus and Philetus, who led people into "further ungodliness" and spread their doctrine "like gangrene" (2 Tim. 2:16–17). Paul condemned them for "saying that the resurrection has already taken place, and they upset the faith of some" (2:18). The Apostle John wrote that "many false prophets have gone out into the world" (1 John 4:1). He also wrote that "many deceivers have gone out into the world, those who do not acknowledge Jesus Christ as coming in the flesh. This is the deceiver and the antichrist" (2 John 7). John also indicated that these deceivers rose up in the midst of the church in his day: "They went out from us, but they were not really of us; for if they had been of us, they would have remained with us; but they went out, so that it would be shown that they all are not of us" (1 John 2:19). All of these Bible passages give us solid scriptural evidence that the words of Jesus were fulfilled in the days of the apostles.

The last warning Jesus gave in Matthew 24:9–12 was that the church would experience increased lawlessness before the coming tribulation. The New Testament writers constantly addressed the sensual living that became prevalent in their time. This worldliness destroyed relationships within the church and tore down the body of Christ. Paul was shocked at the behavior of the members of the Corinthian church: "It is actually reported that there is immorality among you, and immorality of such a kind as does not exist even among the Gentiles, that someone has his father's wife. And you have become arrogant, and have not mourned instead, in order that the one who had done this deed might be removed from your midst" (1 Cor. 5:1–2). Internal and external trials tested the young church.

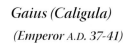

Gaius (Caligula)
(Emperor A.D. 37-41)

Nero (Emperor A.D. 41-54)

Of course, this increase of lawlessness was not confined to the church. A history of the Roman era, especially the history of the Roman emperors, is proof that lawlessness was on the rise. The names Caligula and Nero are synonymous with "lawlessness."

> **"But the one who endures to the end, he will be saved." Matthew 24:13**

Here Jesus offered His disciples comfort. He told them that all those who endure to the end of this great social, religious, and political upheaval would be saved—that is, they would not die in Rome's war with the Jews. What was "the end"? It was not the end of the physical world, but the end of the old covenant that would culminate in the destruction of the temple before that generation passed away.

Jesus' disciples understood that this end was near and that it signified the end of the distinctly Jewish era. Jesus had made it clear to the religious leaders of His day that the kingdom of God would be taken away from them to be "given to a people producing the fruit of it" (Matt. 21:43). The chief priests and Pharisees "understood that He was speaking about *them*" (21:45). *Their* generation would experience the kingdom transfer. For them it was "the end." The Apostle Paul confirmed this realization in his letter to the first-century church at Corinth, when he said that the "ends of the ages" had come upon *them* (1 Cor. 10:11). Peter writes that "end of all things *is at hand*" (1 Peter 4:7).

> **"This gospel of the kingdom shall be preached in the whole world as a testimony to all the nations, and then the end will come." Matthew 24:14**

Many people stumble over this verse, stating that there is no way the gospel was preached in the whole world before A.D. 70. Our first commitment is to believe what the Bible tells us. Remember that 24:34 reads, *"this generation* will not pass away until *all these things take place."* "All these things" must refer to what Jesus says in verse 14.

The word translated "world" in many translations is the Greek word *oikoumene,* "the inhabited earth," the "known world" of the Roman Empire. The same Greek word is used in Luke 2:1: "Now in those days a decree went out from Caesar Augustus, that a census be taken of all *the inhabited earth."* This translation helps us understand that Jesus was saying that the gospel would be preached throughout the Roman Empire before He would return in judgment upon Jerusalem and the temple.

After Jesus' death and resurrection, the gospel did go forth throughout the world. Paul wrote that the gospel "has come to you, just as in all the world also it is constantly bearing fruit and increasing" and that it "was proclaimed in *all creation under heaven"* (Col. 1:6, 23). In Romans, Paul said that the gospel was

The Apostle Paul

"being proclaimed throughout the whole world" (Rom. 1:8). Paul uses the more comprehensive Greek word *kosmos* in Colossians 1:6 and Romans 1:8. Paul was even making plans to go to Spain (Rom. 15:24, 28). It's possible that a church already existed there. This would mean that the gospel had nearly reached the western border of the Roman Empire. Paul quoted from Psalm 19:4: "But I say, surely they have never heard, have they? Indeed they have; 'Their voice has gone out into all the earth, and their words to the ends of the world [*oikoumene*]'" (Rom. 10:18; see also 2 Tim. 4:17). Paul could say that the gospel "has been made known *to all the nations*" (Rom. 16:26). Paul writes to Timothy that Jesus had been "proclaimed among the nations" and "believed on in the world [*kosmos*]" (1 Tim. 3:16).

"Therefore when you see the Abomination of Desolation which was spoken of through Daniel the prophet, standing in the holy place (let the reader understand), then those who are in Judea must flee to the mountains." Matthew 24:15–16

By comparing this passage with the parallel passage in Luke 21:20–21, we can pinpoint the time when the abomination of desolation was to appear: "When you see Jerusalem surrounded by armies, then recognize that her desolation is at hand. Then let those who are in Judea flee to the mountains" Was Jerusalem ever surrounded by armies prior to A.D. 70? Yes! Did many of those who remained in Judea flee the city to save themselves from the impending judgment? Yes!

What was this "abomination of desolation"? Jesus referred His listeners to Daniel 9:27: "And he will make a firm covenant with the many for one week, but in the middle of the week he will put a stop to sacrifice and grain offering; and on the wing of abominations will come one who makes desolate, even until a complete destruction, one that is decreed, is poured out on the one who makes desolate." An abomination in the Old Testament was anything that desecrated the true worship of God (Lev. 7:18 and Deut. 17:1). It is clear that in Jesus' day the Jewish leaders had departed from the true worship of God.

There are several theories on what exactly the "abomination" was. The first theory is that the Zealots—who advocated political and religious freedom from Rome—created the abomination of desolation when they stormed and occupied the temple area, allowed criminals to roam about in the Holy of Holies, and even murdered people within the temple. In the winter of A.D. 67–68, the abomination climaxed with the farcical investiture of the clown Phanni as high priest.[18]

The second theory is that the Romans caused the abomination of desolation when they overtook and burned the temple in A.D. 70. While the sanctuary was still burning, Roman soldiers set up their legionary standards—symbols of Rome—in the temple and offered sacrifices there. The Jews would have viewed this action as the fulfillment of Daniel's vision when the burnt offering ceased and the abomination of desolation was set up. In addition, Luke's description of Jerusalem surrounded by armies— which would have been Roman armies—appears to affirm this theory of a Roman abomination.

In terms of the spiritual covenant between God and His people, the people who were most condemned for defiling the temple were the Jews. Only someone posing as a representative of God could actually defile the worship of God: the corrupt priesthood of Israel. After Jesus' death, the sacrifices of apostate Judaism were an abomination since they denied the atoning work of Christ. The action of the high priest, "standing in the holy place" (24:15), continuing to offer sacrifices in the temple, was an abomination, a rejection of the work of Christ.

While the exact meaning of the "abomination of desolation" is still a matter of debate, Scripture makes it clear that it occurred soon after Jerusalem was surrounded by armies to those living in the first century: "Therefore when *you see* the abomination of desolation" (24:15). As history attests, Jerusalem was surrounded just prior to the temple's destruction in the fall of A.D. 70. Those living in Jerusalem at that time were able to see it. The abomination, whatever it was, brought desolation.

"Then those who are in Judea must flee to the mountains; whoever is on the housetop must not go down to get the things out that are in his house. Whoever is in the field must not turn back to get his cloak. But woe to those who are pregnant and to those who are nursing babies in those days! But pray that your flight will not be in the winter, or on a Sabbath."
Matthew 24:16–20

In these verses, Jesus told His disciples that when the temple's approaching desolation became evident, it would be time for them to head for the hills. The first-century Christians had been expecting the temple's destruction. They had been warned about its impending destruction. The New Testament—which is composed mostly of letters written to first-century churches—is filled with time texts that emphasize that "the end of all things is near" (1 Peter 4:7).

Matthew 24:16–20 presents a clear picture of the customs of first-century Israel. Most roofs were flat with an outside staircase (Mark 2:4; Acts 10:9). They were designed for occupancy (Deut. 22:8), storage (Joshua 2:6), and rest in the evening (2 Sam. 11:2). In addition, Jesus refers to the strict Sabbath laws that were in effect at that time. An acceptable distance for travel on the Sabbath was about three-quarters of a mile as determined by Pharisaical law

(Acts 1:12)—not enough distance to get out of harm's way if a person had to flee the city in an emergency.

History teaches that Christian Jews did indeed heed Jesus' warning before the armies of Titus had captured the city. The Jews who remained were slaughtered. Estimates put the number killed at over one million! Thousands more were taken into captivity. Forty years earlier, Jesus had given the warning to flee to the mountains when Jerusalem was encompassed by armies. Those who believed the prophecy and acted upon it escaped with their lives. Those who remained suffered untold misery.

The judgment is obviously local since in order to escape, a person only had to flee to the mountains of Judea (Matt. 24:16). If this were a world-wide conflagration, there would be no place to escape.

"For then there will be a great tribulation, such as has not occurred since the beginning of the world until now, nor ever will." Matthew 24:21

Some Bible commentators claim that Jesus could not have been referring to the tribulation that led up to and included the fall of Jerusalem in A.D. 70 because that event was not the worst tribulation of all time.

Once again, we must remember that Matthew 24:34 clearly says that all these things would happen in "this generation," that is, the generation to whom Jesus was speaking at that time. The language Jesus used in verse 21 is used elsewhere in Scripture to describe extraordinary events related to judgment and calamity (Ex. 11:6; Ezek. 5:9; Dan. 9:12; 12:1; Joel 2:2; Rev. 16:18). These passages describe calamitous events in terms of superlatives, stating that they were the worst that would ever happen. It is clear that the purpose of hyperbole in all these passages is to emphasize the disastrous nature of each event. This is especially true in Ezekiel 5:9 where we are told that because of Israel's abominations God destroyed the temple and judged the nation in a way that He had "not done, and the like of which I will never do again." This happened hundreds of years before the temple's *second* destruction in A.D. 70.

Furthermore, the tribulation that came upon the temple and the city of Jerusalem was the most dreadful and horrifying. Why? Because this tribulation was the result of the greatest crime against God in all history: crucifying God's promised Redeemer. No other crime was as heinous as killing the "Lord of glory" (1 Cor. 2:8; compare with Luke 24:20; Acts 3:12–26; 1 Thess. 2:15). Consider these few passages regarding the Jews who rejected Jesus:

• "The blood of all the prophets, shed since the foundation of the world, may be charged against this generation, from the blood of Abel to the blood of Zechariah, who was killed between the altar and the house of God; yes, I tell you, it shall be charged against this generation" (Luke 11:50–51)

• "So they cried out, 'Away with Him, away with Him, crucify Him!' Pilate said to them, 'Shall I crucify your King?' The chief priests answered, 'We have no king but Caesar'" (John 19:15).

• "When Pilate saw that he was accomplishing nothing, but rather that a riot was starting, he took water and washed his hands in front of the crowd, saying, 'I am innocent of this Man's blood; see to that yourselves!' And all the people said, 'His blood shall be on us and on our children!' Then he released Barabbas for them; but after having Jesus scourged, he handed Him over to be crucified" (Matthew 27:24–26).

45

"When Pilate saw that he was accomplishing nothing... he took water and washed his hands in front of the crowd, saying, 'I am inocent of this man's blood...'"
(Matt. 27:24)

The severity of the punishment and the hyperbolic language used by Jesus is evidence of the severity of the crime. Israel had broken the demands of the covenant: faith-filled obedience brings life, while faith-less disobedience brings judgment and death (Deut. 28). The rejection of Jesus as God's promised Anointed Savior brought down God's covenant wrath upon all those who rejected Him. The chief priests and elders of the people rejected Jesus, and these were His parting words as He left the temple: "Behold, your house is being left to you desolate! For I say to you, from now on you shall not see Me until you say, 'Blessed is He who comes in the name of the Lord!'" (Matt. 23:38–39).

When Jesus left the temple for the last time, He was leaving it empty and desolate. Just as when the Shekinah glory departed from the temple in Ezekiel 8–11, the temple was left desolate. The desolate temple was shortly filled with demons (Luke 11:20–26). What was spiritually true in A.D. 30 became visibly true in A.D. 70: the temple and the city were made a desolation. The Bible teaches this in no uncertain terms. Jesus told His disciples that all these things would happen to "this generation."

"Unless those days had been cut short, no life [lit. flesh] would have been saved; but for the sake of the elect those days will be cut short." Matthew 24:22

Titus sacking the Temple in Jerusalem

One of the first things we should recognize about Jesus' words here is that He was telling His disciples that the tribulation that was coming would be shortened: "but for the sake of the elect those days will be cut short." Who were the elect Jesus spoke of here? They were Jewish Christians—those who embraced Jesus as the promised and long-awaited Messiah. The tribulation of A.D. 70 was so severe that if God had allowed the Romans to continue their devastation, not a single Jew living in Judea would have survived. For the Romans, these Christian Jews were not considered a separate religious class but simply Jews to be hunted down and killed. For their sake, God cut the tribulation period short.

The use of "all flesh" does not mean everybody in the world either at that time or in some distant time. The use of "all" is often a reference to all without distinction rather than all without exception. Paul writes that at his "first defense no one supported me, but all deserted me; may it not be counted against them" (2 Tim. 4:16). Previously he wrote in the same letter, "all who are in Asia turned away from me, among whom are Phygelus and Hermongenes" (1:15). "[A]ccording to the context, *pasa sarx* ('all flesh'] . . . must be understood of Judea and Jerusalem. Cf. Jer. 12:12 where a similar expression designates the inhabitants of Judea."[19] "All flesh" does not always mean every person without exception, that is, everybody alive in the entire world at any given time. Consider how "all flesh" is used in Acts: "But *this* is what was spoken of through the prophet Joel, . . . 'That I will pour forth of My Spirit upon *all flesh*'" (Acts 2:16–17). The context makes it clear that "all flesh" is a reference to all types of people: sons and daughters, young men and old men, and bond-slaves, both men and women. Not everyone without exception, but everyone without distinction, Jews as well as Gentiles. "'All mankind' seems to be defined by what follows: old and young, women as well as men."[20]

"Then if anyone says to you, 'Behold, here is the Christ,' or 'There He is,' do not believe him. For false

> **Christs and false prophets will arise and show great
> signs and wonders, so as to mislead, if possible, even
> the elect. Behold, I have told you in advance. So if they
> say to you, 'Behold, He is in the wilderness,' do not
> go out, or, 'Behold, He is in the inner rooms,' do not
> believe them." Matthew 24:23–26**

Here Jesus again alludes to the false prophets who would be a part of the tribulation of that period. He had spoken of false prophets before, in verse 11, but in all likelihood, Jesus was indicating that there would be an interval of time between the first wave of false prophets and the second. Jesus told His disciples that shortly after His ascension false christs and prophets would appear, "but that is not yet the end" (24:6). Then, as the time for the destruction of Jerusalem drew closer, and as the time for that generation would come to an end, more false prophets would arise.

The unbelieving Jews of Jesus' day had rejected their Messiah and instead looked for a political savior to overthrow the tyrants of Rome (John 6:15). These deluded people would continue to look for a political messiah right up until the time of Jerusalem's destruction. This wishful thinking made people willing to embrace an increasing number of messianic figures in hopes of being delivered from Roman oppression. In times of trouble, people look for even a glimmer of hope for securing deliverance. The Israelites' true hope was to embrace Jesus as the Messiah. Their Messiah had come, but they rejected and crucified Him. That is why they believed every false prophet who came along promising redemption.

> **"For just as the lightening comes from the east and
> flashes even to the west, so will the coming of the Son
> of Man be." Matthew 24:27**

Jesus told His people that He would come "just as lightening comes from the east," that is, quickly and without warning. In the Bible, lightening often signifies the presence of the Lord or His coming in judgment (Ex. 19:16; 20:18; Job 36:30; Ezek. 21:15, 28; Zech. 9:14). God was not physically present during any of these Old Testament comings, but His presence was obvious. Deuteronomy 33:2 says, "The Lord came from Sinai, and dawned on them from Seir; He shone forth from Mount Paran, and He came from the midst of ten thousand holy ones; at His right hand there was flashing lightening for them." Was God physically present during these times? No. Did He really come? Most certainly!

In Matthew 24:27, Jesus indicated that He would participate in Jerusalem's destruction. The Roman armies led by Titus would act as God's agents to set the temple on fire. In the Old Testament,

Titus bringing Jewish captives to Rome

pagan Assyria had been sent by God to judge the Israelites who had turned away from Him. Assyria was called the "rod of My anger, and the staff in whose hands is My indignation" (Isa. 10:5). In a similar way, Rome was the tool Jesus would use to punish apostate Israel in A.D. 70. In Luke 23:28–30, Jesus told the "daughters of Jerusalem" to "weep for yourselves and your children." No future generation was in view here. Once again we are introduced to a local judgment. A lightning strike is not seen around the world. Its sight line is from horizon to horizon.

"Wherever the corpse is, there the vultures will gather." Matthew 24:28

Being familiar with the Hebrew Scriptures, Jesus' disciples would have understood exactly what He was saying here. They would have recognized the words of Jeremiah judging those who break God's covenant: "The dead bodies of this people will be food for the birds of the sky and for the beasts of the earth" (Jer. 7:33). And stated later in Jeremiah, "[God] will cause them to fall by the sword before their enemies and by the hand of those who seek their life; and I will give over their carcasses as food for the birds of the sky and the beasts of the earth" (19:7).

Jesus was acting out in word and deeds the prophecies given to Jeremiah centuries before. Notice the similarities between what Jeremiah did and what Jesus did. Jeremiah was told to "stand in the gate of the Lord's house" and proclaim God's Word to the people (Jer. 7:2). Compare this with Matthew 23:36 and 24:1 where Jesus was preaching at the gate of the temple. In the days of Jeremiah, just as in Jesus' day, the people were told not to trust in the temple and empty rituals (Jer. 7:4). The temple was meaningless without obedience: "Thus says the Lord of hosts, the God of Israel, 'Amend your ways and your deeds, and I will let you dwell in this place'" (7:3). Without obedience, the temple had "become a den of robbers" (Jer. 7:11; compare with Matt. 21:13). Therefore, God rejected "the generation of His wrath" (Jer. 7:29b; compare with Matt. 23:36; 24:34).

The Jerusalem of Jesus' day, because of its dead rituals, was a carcass, food for the scavenging birds, the Roman armies. In addition, there was a literal fulfillment of this prophecy in that tens of thousands of people were killed during the Roman siege. (The historian Josephus says there were over a million deaths.) Even the temple area was not spared. The Idumean and Zealot revolt left thousands slaughtered in and around the temple. A single carcass would have rendered the city and temple area "unclean," and, according to Number 19:11–22, anyone touching the corpse of a human being was unclean and must be cut off from Israel. As our High Priest, Jesus could no longer remain in the city because of its defilement. It had to be burned with fire for purification.

On the Mount of Olives, the disciples came to Jesus to point out the temple buildings, and Jesus condemned that temple as spiritually empty and defiled, fit only for destruction. But He promised that just as certainly as He would destroy that temple, He would raise up another perfect temple in three days—the temple of His body (see John 2:19–21). Therefore, all Jesus' disciples must now point out the new temple to all those who seek salvation.

"But immediately after the tribulation of those days the sun will be darkened, and the moon will not give its light and the stars will fall from the sky and the powers of the heavens will be shaken."
Matthew 24:29

The tribulation Jesus spoke of in verse 29 was the culmination of events that took place just prior to the destruction of Jerusalem in A.D. 70. Jesus said that *immediately* after this tribulation, the sun and moon would be darkened, the stars would fall, etc. So, whatever these images mean, we know that they followed "immediately after" the tribulation described in verses 15–28. Matthew used the word "immediately" to indicate that there would not be a delay or postponement (see how "immediately" is used elsewhere in Matthew: 3:16; 4:20, 22; 8:3; 20:34; 21:19; and 26:74). Jesus' disciples were not asking about the end of the world (*kosmos*), but about the end of that covenant age (*aion*). When the tribulation of "those days' was completed, the end of the temple and city would be near at hand. As the time for Jerusalem's demise drew closer, other signs would appear. These later signs were described by Jesus as the sun darkening, the moon not giving light, stars falling, and the powers of the heavens shaking.

What did Jesus mean by this imagery? Did the sun literally become darkened and did the moon literally cease reflecting the light from the sun? The language used by Jesus is typical of Old Testament imagery where stellar phenomena represent kings and kingdoms. Let's begin at the beginning. The first chapter of Genesis shows us why the Bible compares the sun, moon, and stars to rulers and their kingdoms: The sun ("greater light") and the moon ("lesser light") are said to *govern* the day and night (Gen. 1:16). Later in Genesis, in Joseph's dream, "the sun and the moon and eleven stars" bow down to him (37:9). Joseph's family immediately understood the significance of the images, that Joseph's father, mother, and brothers would bow down to him. The sun, moon, and stars represent Israel.

Elsewhere in the Bible, stars are often used to symbolize earthly rulers and governments (see Judges 5:19–20), and, in particular, Israel (see Gen. 22:17; 26:4; Deut. 1:10). There is no mistaking the stellar imagery of Revelation 12:1–2: "And a great sign appeared in heaven: a woman clothed with the sun, and the moon under her feet, and on her head a crown of twelve stars; and she was with child; and she cried out, being in labor and in pain to give birth." This likeness is a picture of Israel in all her glory giving birth to the Messiah, the long awaited Savior of Israel and the world.

Throughout the Bible, solar, lunar, and stellar language is used to depict great political and social upheaval (e.g., Isa. 13:9–11; Ezek. 32:7–8). Using stellar language to indicate political or social significance has continued even to the present day. Many nations use symbols of stars in their flags. We also speak of people's success or failure as "a rising star" or "his star is fallen."

Just as in Revelation 12, Matthew 24:29 combines the imagery of the sun, moon, and stars to describe Israel as a nation. Jesus spoke of the sun and moon going dark and the stars falling to indicate the coming judgment of the nation of Israel. Keep in mind that verse 34 is the time text that governs verse 29, as well as all the other verses that precede verse 34; this judgment would occur within a generation of Jesus' conversation with His disciples.

The Old Testament—the only Scriptures the disciples had as a revelational reference point—is replete with metaphors of the darkening of sun and moon and the falling of stars. In each of these cases, the images clearly indicate the fall of nations.

Let's first look at a passage that speaks of the destruction of Babylon by the Medes: "Behold, the day of the Lord is coming, cruel, with fury and burning anger, to make the land a desolation; and He will exterminate its sinners from it. For the stars of heaven and their constellations will not flash forth their light; the sun will be dark when it rises, and the moon will not shed its light" (Isa. 13:9–10).

Similar language is used to describe the destruction of Egypt: "And when I extinguish you, I will cover the heavens and darken their stars; I will cover the sun with a cloud, and the moon will not give its light. All the shining lights in the heavens I will darken over you and will set darkness on your land" (Ezek. 32:7–8).

Even more telling, this kind of stellar imagery was also used to indicate the judgment of Israel. "Alas, you who are longing for the day of the Lord, for what purpose will the day of the Lord be to you? It will be darkness and not light" (Amos 5:18). And again, "It will come about in that day, declares the Lord God, that I shall make the sun go down at noon and make the earth dark in broad daylight" (8:9). Using similar language, in Matthew 24:29, Jesus told His disciples that there would come a time of intense divine judgment against Israel within that generation.

"And then the sign of the Son of Man will appear in the sky, and then all the tribes of the earth will mourn, and they will see the Son of Man coming on the clouds of the sky with power and great glory."
Matthew 24:30

This verse is often interpreted to mean the physical Second Coming of Christ at the end of history. We must remember that this verse, like all the others we have discussed thus far, is governed by the time text of verse 34: "this generation will not pass away until all these things take place." We must again let the Bible be our guide to the interpretation of this type of biblical imagery. What did Jesus mean when He spoke of the Son of Man coming on clouds? Throughout the Bible, God often showed Himself by the physical presence of clouds, even though no one ever saw Him (Ex. 13:21; 14:24; 19:9; 20:21; 33:9; 34:5; 1 Kings 8:12). In addition, the Bible constantly refers to clouds in reference to God's judgment: the "day of the Lord . . . will be a day of clouds" (Ezek. 30:3; Joel 2:1–2); "In whirlwind and storm is His way, and clouds are the dust beneath His feet" (Nahum 1:3). In addition, many verses describe God "coming on the clouds" to indicate His judgment: "Behold, the Lord is riding on a swift cloud, and is about to come to Egypt" (Isa. 19:1; see also Psalm 104:3–4).

In each of the above examples, clouds are symbols of God's presence—either His salvation or His judgment—and in no instance are symbolic of God's physical presence. Why should the descriptive events of Matthew 24:30 mean something different?

The most powerful Old Testament reference for Matthew 24:30 is found in Daniel 7:13–14, because it is the passage that Jesus quoted. Daniel 7:13 says, "I kept looking in the night vision, and behold, with the clouds of heaven one like a Son of Man was coming, and He came up to the Ancient of Days and was presented before Him." Notice that the coming of the Son of Man here is not *down* but *up*. The perspective is from heaven, and the Son of Man is coming up to God the Father to receive the kingdom. With this in mind, it is clear that in Matthew 24:30 Jesus was describing to His disciples His powerful and triumphal enthronement, as He would display righteous victory over His enemies.

Jesus' victorious description here in Matthew 24:30 matches the words He would later speak to the high priest at His trial, that he would see "the Son of Man sitting at the right hand of power and coming on the clouds of heaven" (Matt. 26:64). Jesus was speaking of His ascension, when He would go up "with the clouds of heaven" to receive the kingdom from His Father (Mark 16:19; Acts 1:9–11).

The focus is on Jesus as the Christ and His kingdom. Under the Old Covenant, the kingdom had belonged to the Jews, but many rejected Jesus, so the kingdom would be "taken away from [them] and given to a people producing the fruit of it" (Matt. 21:43). An essential part of Jesus' enthronement was the covenant transfer of the kingdom from the unbelieving Jews to the universal church, made up of believing Jews and Gentiles. The destruction of Jerusalem in A.D. 70 marked this transfer, and it marked the establishment of Jesus as King over His world-wide kingdom. Jesus was given "dominion, glory and a kingdom, that all the peoples, nations, and men of every language might serve Him" (Dan. 7:14), and the generation of Jews who rejected their King would live to regret it when they remained in Jerusalem and suffered under Roman oppression.

At first reading, many assume that in Matthew 24:30 Jesus was saying that everyone on earth would see Him physically appearing in the sky, and part of this assumption stems from a poor translation of the text. First of all, the text does not speak of *Jesus* appearing in the *sky*. A word-for-word translation of the Greek reads, "And then will appear the *sign* of the Son of Man *in heaven*." Jesus was telling His disciples to look for the sign of His enthronement in heaven. The destruction of the city of Jerusalem pointed the way to the New Jerusalem. All Christians now look to "the Jerusalem above" (Gal. 4:26).

The second bit of confusion is the phrase "all the tribes of the *earth* will mourn" which is more accurately translated "all the tribes of the *land* will mourn." Jesus was warning His audience to flee Judea when they saw "Jerusalem surrounded by armies" (Luke 21:20). Only those near enough to the temple would be able to see the "abomination of desolation . . . standing in the holy place" (Matt. 24:15). The Olivet Discourse was clearly not a message to the world, but rather a warning to the tribes of Israel of the first century. The tribes of Israel mourned because they understood that judgment was near. They must either embrace the Messiah or perish in the conflagration. The Jews who rejected Jesus because He was not a political savior died at the hands of the Roman army. Their Savior had come, and they had crucified Him forty years earlier. Those who "pierced" Jesus (Zech. 12:10; John 19:37; Rev. 1:7) experienced His covenant wrath.[21]

But when did "they see the Son of Man coming on the clouds of heaven with power and great glory" (Matt. 24:30)? Obviously before that first-century generation passed away. The language is very similar to what Jesus tells Nathanael: "And [Jesus] said to [Nathanael], 'Truly, truly, I say to you, you shall see the heavens opened, and the angels of God ascending and descending upon the Son of Man'"

(John 1:51). The Greek word for "see" in John 1:51 is the same word used in Matthew 24:30 (*horaō*). "Although Jesus is address-ing Nathanael, the 'you' to whom he promises the vision of v. 51 is plural: the vision is probably for all the disciples, and by extension, for those also who would follow them."[22] When did Nathanael and those with him "see" what Jesus said they would see? It's possible that they actually did see what Jesus described but the event is not recorded in Scripture. Matthew Henry, in his commentary on this passage, states the following comment: "There were many things

Matthew Henry (1662-1714)

which Christ did, and those in the presence of his disciples, which were not written (John 20:30), and why not this?" Therefore it's possible that at the time of Jerusalem's judgment and the temple's destruction, the Jews saw Jesus coming on the clouds of heaven, that is, the heavens opened and they saw Jesus enthroned in heaven.

> **"And He will send forth His angels with a great**
> **trumpet and they will gather together His elect from**
> **the four winds, from one end of the sky to the other."**
> **Matthew 24:31**

In the context of the chapter, and in the context of verse 34 ("this generation will not pass away until all these things take place"), it becomes evident that verse 31 is not a reference to the end of the physical world but rather the spread of the gospel to the nations of the world.

The Greek word translated "angels" (*angelos*) is used throughout the Bible for human "messengers" (2 Chron. 26:15–16; Haggai 1:13; Mal. 2:7; 3:1; Matt. 11:10; Mark 1:2; Luke 7:24, 27; Luke 9:52; James 2:25). With this in mind, some commentators interpret Jesus as saying that after the judgment of Jerusalem His messengers would preach the gospel of the new covenant far beyond the confines of the Roman Empire. While this is a possible interpretation, R.T. France, who once argued this way, now thinks "it more likely that angels are here credited with a 'missionary' role in the ingathering of God's people; cf. the description of angels in Heb. 1:14 as ['*Are they not all ministering spirits, sent out to render service for the sake of those who will inherit salvation?*']."[23]

The phrase "from the four winds" is a reference to the entire world. Indeed, the phrase "the four corners of the earth" is a common expression even to this day. Jesus was emphasizing the fact that under the new covenant, His elect are gathered from everywhere.

The "great trumpet" is the call of the gospel. It recalls Numbers 10:1–10 where silver trumpets were made to call the people together for worship and to set them on their march. It also refers to the year of Jubilee, the year when the world reverts to its original owners, the year when Satan is dispossessed and Christ reclaims the world (Acts 3:19–21). The Jubilee year signified the coming of Christ's kingdom, and it was announced by trumpets (Lev. 25:8–17; Luke 4:16–21; Isa. 61:1–3). The voice of the messengers of the gospel acts similar to the sound of a trumpet calling the people to repentance; "Cry loudly, do not hold back; raise your voice like a trumpet, and declare to My people their transgression and to the house of Jacob their sins" (Isa. 58:1; see also Jer. 6:1; Ezek. 33:3-6; Rom. 10:18).

The trumpet is also used to bring the nation together as a unified people: "And it will come about in that day, that the LORD will start His threshing from the flowing stream of the Euphrates to the brook of Egypt; and *you will be gathered up one by one*, O sons of Israel. It will come about also in that day that *a great trumpet will be blown*; and those who were perishing in the land of Assyria and who were scattered in the land of Egypt will come and worship the LORD in the holy mountain at Jerusalem" (Isa. 27:12–13). Isaiah's gathering is not a modern-day, world-wide gathering since the gathering is limited to those lands around Israel. The gathering is from the land of Assyria to the land of Egypt, the places where the Jews had been taken to and held in captivity. Edward J. Young writes: "Such figurative language symbolizes the call for return. We are not to conceive of a literal trumpet being blown."[24]

Matthew 24:31 draws upon Old Testament imagery to symbolize the great work about to commence, the great gathering of God's people into a new nation. The word for "gather" is the Greek word *synagogue*. A gathering of Jews met in a synagogue, but Judaism rejected Christ and had become a "synagogue of Satan" (Rev. 2:9). The true synagogue of God—the church—is made up of believing Jews and Gentiles from around the world.

"Now learn the parable from the fig tree: when its branch has already become tender, and puts forth its leaves, you know that summer is near; even so you too, when you see all these things, recognize that He is near, right at the door." Matthew 24:32–33

Contrary to what some dispensational Bible commentators say, Jesus used the parable of the fig tree as a simple analogy. He pointed out that when leaves begin to sprout on a fig tree—or, for that matter, on any tree (Luke 21:29–30)—it is a sign that summer is near. In a similar way, when Jesus' followers saw these signs, they would know that Jesus was near, "right at the door." Near to what? Near to fulfilling the promise He made about coming within a generation to destroy the temple. This is the simple and clear meaning of the text. Any other interpretation wildly stretches the text beyond its intended meaning.

"Truly I say to you, this generation will not pass away until all these things take place." Matthew 24:34

With this verse we are brought full circle. In a straightforward manner, Jesus made it clear that all the events outlined in the preceding verses would be fulfilled before the passing away of that first-century generation. Luke's account of the Olivet Discourse confirms that the generation Jesus had in mind was the generation to whom He was speaking: "But keep on the alert at all times, praying that you may have strength to escape all these things that are about to take place and to stand before the Son of Man" (Luke 21:36). Once we determine the meaning of "you," we can resolve the meaning of "this generation." Clearly, Jesus was referring to those to whom He spoke, the same group He told to "keep on the alert" and to pray. Jesus confirmed the nearness of the unfolding of the events by telling His listeners that the cataclysm was "about to take place." Without a proper understanding of this key time text, prophetic forecasters will always find Matthew 24 fertile ground for wild speculation.

Conclusion

The clear time references that govern the timing of the Olivet Discourse prophecy—Matthew 23:36 and Matthew 24:34—make it clear that Jesus was speaking of the events leading up to and including the fall of Jerusalem in A.D. 70. Those who manipulate the clear meaning of the phrase "this generation" by trying to make it refer to events in the distant future are involved in prophetic speculation that contributes to last days madness.

In other words, if we abandon the clear time indicators of this passage, then these verses can be applied to any generation. All eras of history have had and will continue to have wars, false prophets, famines, and the like. If people fail to recognize the timing of these events set by Scripture and the historical context of Jesus' words, they will always be led astray to look for some future "great tribulation."

At this point you might be asking, If the Great Tribulation has already happened, then when *will* Jesus return? The only "sign" the Bible gives us is the fullness of the kingdom, "when He has abolished all rule and authority and power. For He must reign until He has put all His enemies under His feet" (1 Cor. 15:24–25). We know that Jesus is presently reigning over the universe from heaven. Heaven is His throne and earth is His footstool (Isa. 66:1). He will continue to reign in this manner until all His enemies are conquered (Psalm 110:1; Acts 2:35). When this is accomplished, Jesus will return to judge the living and the dead. At that time, "the dead in Christ shall rise first. Then we who are alive and remain will be caught up together with them in the clouds to meet the Lord in the air, and so we shall always be with the Lord" (1 Thess. 4:16–17).

The material in this book is a plea for the church to take another look at Bible prophecy, especially as it relates to the end times. Taking an honest, biblical approach to prophecy will open your eyes to deeper truths within Scripture and will guide your attitude to the future.

When Christians are left to wonder whether the great tribulation might occur in their generation, this kind of speculation often leads to a pessimistic view of society, Christian activism, and the future. However, once we realize that the Great Tribulation has already come, and that the church has been promised a progressively victorious future, we will be encouraged to work diligently for the sake of Christ and His kingdom. Let us not forget that we serve the victorious King who has been given "dominion, glory and a kingdom, that all the peoples, nations, and men of every language might serve Him" (Dan. 7:14).

NOTES

1.   Subsequent revised editions are published under the *Oxford Scofield Study Bible.* For a study of the theology of the Scofield Bible, see Albertus Pieters, *The Scofield Bible* (Swengel, PA: Reiner Publications, 1965).

2.   Henry Hammond, *A Paraphrase, and Annotations Upon all the Books of The New Testament, Briefly Explaining all the Difficult Places Thereof* (London: Printed for John Nicholson, at the King's-Arms in Little Britain, 1702), 102.

3.   John Lightfoot, *A Commentary on the New Testament from the Talmud and Hebraica,* 4 vols. (Oxford: Oxford University Press, [1658–1674] 1859), 2:320.

4.   Philip Doddridge, *The Family Expositor; or, A Paraphrase and Version of the New Testament; with Critical Notes, and a Practical Improvement of each Section,* 6 vols. (Charlestown, Mass.: Ethridge and Company, 1807), 1:377.

5.   Thomas Newton, *Dissertations on the Prophecies, Which Have Remarkably Been Fulfilled, and at This Time Are Fulfilling in the World* (London: J. F. Dove, 1754), 377.

6.   John Gill, *An Exposition of the New Testament,* 3 vols. (London: Mathews and Leigh, 1809), 1:296.

7. Thomas Scott, *The Holy Bible Containing the Old and New Testaments, Containing the Old and New Testaments, According to the Authorized Version; with Explanatory Notes, Practical Observations, and Copious Marginal References*, 3 vols. (New York: Collins and Hannay, 1832), 3:111.

8. Tim LaHaye and Thomas Ice, *Charting the End Times: A Visual Guide to Understanding Bible Prophecy* (Eugene, OR: Harvest House Publishers, 2001), 36.

9. Tim LaHaye, gen. ed., *Prophecy Study Bible* (Chattanooga, TN: AMG Publishers, 2000), 1040, note on Matthew 24:34.

10. R. T. France, *The Gospel According to Matthew: An Introduction and Commentary* (Downers Grove, IL: InterVarsity Press, 1985), 337. John Nolland makes the same point: "In the Greek text 'your coming' and 'the completion of the age' are marked as belonging together by sharing a single definite article" (*The Gospel of Matthew: A Commentary on the Greek Text* [Grand Rapids, MI: Eerdmans, 2005], 961).

11. Flavius Josephus, *The Antiquities of the Jews* in *The Works of Josephus*, trans. William Whiston (Peabody, MA: Hendrickson Publishers, 1987), 20:5:1, 531.

12. Newton, *Dissertations on the Prophecies*, 332–333.

13. Larry Spargimino, "How Preterists Misuse History to Advance Their View of Prophecy," *The End Times Controversy: The Second Coming Under Attack*, eds. Tim LaHaye and Thomas Ice (Eugene, OR: Harvest House, 2003), 210.

14. Tacitus, *The Annals of Imperial Rome*, trans. Michael Grant (London: Penguin Books, 1989), 271.

15. Josephus, *The Wars of the Jews* in *The Works of Josephus*, 5:12:3, 723.

16. Quoted in Thomas Scott, *The Holy Bible Containing the Old and New Testaments, According to the Authorized Version; with Explanatory Notes, Practical Observations, and Copious Marginal References*, 3 vols. (New York: Collins and Hannay, 1832), 3:108.

17. George Edmundson, *The Church in Rome in the First Century* (London: Longmans, Green and Co., 1913), 143.

18. Josephus, *The Wars of the Jews* in *The Works of Josephus* 4:36–10 and 4:5:4, 671–172, 680.

19. William L. Lane, *Commentary on the Gospel of Mark* (Grand Rapids, MI: Eerdmans, 1974), 471 n. 82.

20. Everett F. Harrison, *Acts the Expanding Church* (Chicago: Moody Press, 1975), 58.

21. For a discussion of Zechariah 12:10, see Gary DeMar, *Zechariah 12 and the "Esther Connection"* (Powder Springs, GA: American Vision, 2005), 16–24.

22. D. A. Carson, *The Gospel According to John* (Grand Rapids, MI: Eerdmans, 1991), 163.

23. R. T. France, *The Gospel of Mark* (Grand Rapids, MI: Eerdmans, 2002), 536–537.

24. Edward J. Young, *The Book of Isaiah*, 3 vols. (Grand Rapids, MI: Eerdmans, 1970), 2:19.

Eschatology Resources for Further Study

Visit *www.AmericanVision.org* for prices and
detailed descriptions of these books!

CATALOG #	PRODUCT
DVD-ACPF	Abrahamic Covenant: Postponed or Fulfilled? (DVD)
BKP-4700	An Evening in Ephesus with John, the Son of Zebedee
BKH-0000	Armageddon Now! (Hardback – Limited Edition)
BKP-0575	Armageddon Now! (Paperback)
BKH-0700	Back to the Future (Hardback): A Study on the Book of Revelation
DVD-BTUP	Basic Training for Understanding Bible Prophecy (DVD Series)
BKP-0419	Beast of Revelation
DVD-BORI	Beast of Revelation Identified (DVD)
BKP-0435	Before Jerusalem Fell
BKP-0893	Biblical Apocalyptics
BKP-0255	Biblical Hermeneutics
BKP-0SMI	Coming of the Lord, the Last Days, and the End of the World
BKP-0337	Darby, Dualism and the Decline of Dispensationalism
BKP-0370	Day and the Hour
BKH-2092	Days of Vengeance
BKH-5583	Early Church and the End of the World
BKP-0429	End Times Fiction
BKP-0145	Foes From the Northern Frontier
KP-0801	Four Views on the Book of Revelation
CDA-GDUF	Gary DeMar Under Fire (Audio CDs)
BKP-CRB4	Gospel of the Kingdom: An Examination of Modern Dispensationalism
BKP-2556	Great Tribulation
BKP-0013	Great Tribulation: Past or Future
BKP-CRB3	Hope of Israel: What Is It?
BKP-0362	Is Jesus Coming Soon?
BKP-040X	Last Days According to Jesus
BKP-0354	Last Days Madness (Fourth Edition)
BKH-0377	Last Disciple
BKH-0487	Last Sacrifice
BKP-CRB1	Message From Patmos
BKH-077X	On the Road to Armageddon
BKP-0521	Paradise Restored
BKP-013X	Parousia
BKP-0709	Perilous Times
BKP-0897	Postmillennialism: An Eschatology of Hope
CDA-0039	Prophecy Works: Volume 1 CD-ROM
BKP-047X	Puritan Hope
BKH-0285	Revelation: Four Views
CDR-0700	Selective Prophecy Works: Volume 1 CD-ROM
BKP-CRB2	Seventy Weeks and the Great Tribulation
BKP-0BRO	Siege and Destruction of Jerusalem
BKP-0M02	Three R's: Rapture, Revisionism, Robbery
BKP-0438	Three Views on the Millennium and Beyond